HOW TO TREAT YOUR BOSS
(AND GET PROMOTED FAST!)

Adebayo S. David

THE CORNERSTONE PUBLISHING

HOW TO TREAT YOUR BOSS

(And Get Promoted Fast!)

Copyright © 2020 by **Adebayo S. David**

ISBN: 978-1-952098-23-9

Published by:
Cornerstone Publishing
A Division of Cornerstone Creativity Group LLC
Info@thecornerstonepublishers.com
www.thecornerstonepublishers.com
516.547.4999

Author's Contact

To book Pastor Bayo to speak at your next event or to order bulk copies of this book please send email to: greaterthingsnow@yahoo.com

CONTENTS

INTRODUCTION

A greater percentage of our lives revolves around work and the workplace. It's either we are getting on a job or moving out of a job. We are either starting a business or getting out of a business. Or it could be that we are starting an organization or getting out of an organization.

Moreover, nobody ever becomes his or her own boss without ever having one. And bosses come in different forms - your parents, teachers, guardians, coach, mentor, pastor or your immediate boss on your present job. Simply put, you are connected to a boss directly or indirectly.

So, how do you relate with your boss and reap the maximum benefits for your promotion and success in life? That's what you are about to discover here. This book is about the unwritten laws and rules for business success and promotion in your career while relating with your boss.

Your boss plays a major role in your promotion and career success; you cannot ignore him. He may not always be right, but he is your boss anyway. So, how you treat him will determine how fast you will rise.

Where there is a boss, there is power. Where there is a boss, there is favor and promotion - either in monetary or positional form.

It's time to learn how to treat your boss right.

Rule 1

APPRECIATE YOUR BOSS (WHETHER HE'S THERE OR NOT!)

There is nothing as powerful as a thankful heart. A thankful heart is always abounding. A thankful heart is graceful. A thankful heart is vibrant. And a thankful heart is always attracting good things to itself. **Honor and promotion will naturally gravitate towards a thankful person.**

Your boss is one of the key reasons you are still on your job and getting the pay and the perks. If there is anything you need to do for him (or her), it is to always appreciate him openly and secretly - not with flattery, but with sincerity of heart.

When was the last time you said to your boss: "Thank you, sir, for allowing me to work in this organization. Thanks for giving me the opportunity and platform to know all l know now. I appreciate you, and wonder what my professional experience would have been without you."?

Say this directly to your boss or to those who are close to him, who he often listens to. When you appreciate your boss, even in his absence, there are those who will blow the trumpet to him about your appreciation of him. Even if he had been considering a negative action against you, he would change his mind and you would rather be promoted.

Remember, others are interested in your job. Never lose your position. Never lose your job. And always be mindful that your boss is instrumental to your retaining that job.

Always appreciate your boss, in his presence and in his absence

Rule 2

CLEAR HIS MESS, BEFORE SHOWING HIM HIS NEMESIS

Some subordinates are full of pride and ego. They would rather want their boss to lose his position than to help him keep it. Thus, they keep expecting him to make a major mistake and then get kicked out.

Once your boss recognizes that you are not watching out for his interest, he will be the first to set you up for termination before you mess him up!

So, if you are going to keep your job and get promoted fast, always try (as much as it's permissible) to fix your boss's mistakes, even before he realizes the mess he could have been in. After you have cleared his mess, you can show him the nemesis he could have been in.

The moment your boss can trust you to clean up after

him, you will always be the first to be considered for promotion.

Always clear your boss's mess before showing him his nemesis!

Rule 3

SOLVE HIS KNOTTY PROBLEMS, WITHOUT CREATING MORE FOR HIM

Nobody likes problems, but everybody has got problems. People don't like to have more problems; rather, they need someone to help solve their problems, without creating more for them.

Whether, you like it or not, your boss has got some problems, too. Executive problems, domestic problems, managerial problems, documentations problems, or financial problems – it could be any. Do your best to locate some of these problems without asking. Sometimes you could ask, depending on your relationship with him.

Once you identify your boss's problems, try to solve

them. Go the extra mile for him. Inconvenience yourself, if necessary, but don't neglect your work. The advantage of this is that it gives you an edge over your colleagues. **Every problem you solve for your boss without creating another will set you on the path of promotion and success.**

Vice President Daniel, during the reign of King Nebuchadnezzar of the Babylonian Empire, helped the king to solve the problem of a forgotten dream that was disturbing and frightening. As soon as Daniel was able to solve this problem by relating the dream to the king and also giving the interpretation, the king promoted him. Daniel didn't forget his three Hebrew friends. They were also promoted!

Why?

• They solved the king's knotty problems.

• You are promoted for the problems you solve and not for the ones you create!

Rule 4

NEVER TRY TO OUTSHINE YOUR BOSS, EVEN WHEN THE SHINE IS IN YOU

Have you ever notice that everybody likes some measure of popularity, superiority and supremacy? That is always the case with your boss. The boss always loves to be the boss. The one who takes all the credit for all the good things in the organization, even though he is not the only one that makes the all the good things happen.

No matter your level of intelligence or excellence, you are not as powerful

as the boss. So, don't draw attention to yourself; keep the focus on the boss.

Jesus kept the focus on God the Father - the biggest Boss of mankind.

Learn from Him. Talk more about your boss.

The boss always wins. The boss always likes to get the attention, the praise, and the accolades. So, if you are going to get promoted fast, never score your own card by yourself. Drop your ego and pride of success, achievement and excellence; just pass it all to the boss. He takes the credit and the shine, while you take the satisfaction of fulfillment as the secret engine that makes the vehicle run. What the people see is the body of the beautiful car; but you are the real thing, man!

To get to the top of your career, work yourself out, without caring who gets the credit. Just give it all to the boss who will eventually work it out as your promotion.

Follow these tips:

1. Never try to outshine the boss. If you do, he may fire you because you are trying to say that he is incompetent. He can do it in a subtle way; all he needs is to capitalize on one minor error from you.

2. Never draw attention of success to yourself; give all the credit to the boss.

3. Never talk more about yourself and all you have done to achieve success. Rather, talk about all the boss has done to make you achieve all the success.

4. Never be the cloud that blocks the radiance from your boss.

5. Always make your boss feel comfortable around you because you like to talk more about him than yourself.

6. Always make your boss appear more brilliant than he is, and you will get your desired promotion and other benefits.

Rule 5

BE MORE PARTICULAR ABOUT YOUR BOSS'S SUCCESS THAN YOURS

General Joab was a mighty man, a great general in the army of the king of Israel. He conquered nations, took cities, made their kings and armies useless. He took mighty crowns and trophies by his skill and strength.

But the most amazing thing about General Joab is that, although he conquered all the cities and the crowns, he never took any for himself; he gave all to King David. Joab put the gold-plated crown on his boss's head through the many wars he won for him.

General Joab was always particular about the success and increase of his master's kingdom rather than his own success. These acts endeared him to King David, and because of this and many other proofs of his loyalty, King David made him his chief of staff. He also got away with many things.

The boss is not too comfortable with subordinates who are too particular about their own personal success. When you act like General Joab, you will get away with a lot of things with your boss.

How much success and promotion do you want? **The easiest route to achieving your career expectations and aspirations is for you to make your boss very successful.** When you do, he will promote you and also give you some connection which may take you beyond your imaginations.

Wait a minute. Do you sometimes worry that the boss might use you and you get nothing in return? Oh no! You should never think that way because whatever you are doing for the boss to be successful, you are also doing for yourself. The fact is that **by making your boss successful, you are building a success database for your personal life.** It is an experience that nobody can take away from you and you can use it anytime, anywhere!

Rule 6

GO THE EXTRA MILE FOR YOUR BOSS

Have you ever asked to help your boss with some little, routine task? Have you ever thought that he may have some issues on his mind that might require only someone close to him to help? Perhaps you have never thought you should ask him or lend a helping hand.

Sometimes we think that, after all, we are on a job to get paid for what we are employed to do! Yeah! But that could be wrong!

Every time you get on a job, there are other hidden duties that you may be required to do which are not written down as part of your job specification. You need to identify them and do them as they form part of your unseen appraisals for your promotion.

So, you may need to sometimes ask the boss, "What can I do for you, sir?" When you learn to stretch yourself to do some "extra" jobs for the boss, you are qualifying yourself for a promotion.

Think about walking him down to his car. Think about decluttering his table or helping to remove his bin by calling the cleaner. An extra mile for the boss's comfort will not be a bad choice; rather, it will enhance your promotion.

Spend a little extra time with him after closing hours. Get to the office before him if you can. This will speak volume for you towards your promotion.

Note, however, that some caution is needed, when it comes closeness with a boss that is of the opposite gender to you. Too much closeness could be misinterpreted by either the boss himself or others around – especially your spouse, if you are married. So, be discreet and disciplined, even as you seek to go the extra mile for your boss.

Rule 7

NEVER EQUATE YOURSELF WITH YOUR BOSS

Practice the principle of inequality.

It doesn't matter how you look, how much you know or what your family background is - your boss is always the boss!

If you are going to get to the top of your career, you must stay humble before your boss. You are not equal to your boss, no matter the level of your exposure. The boss is always the boss!

To equate yourself with your boss is to call for your own downfall.

The boss is your superior and you are his subordinate. Every subordinate who tries to equate himself with the boss will never last in an organization. If you are fortunate, you may be redeployed; otherwise you are on your way out.

Here are few tips:

1. Always take the lowly place before the boss.
2. Never run your mouth while the boss is speaking.
3. Let the boss always have the final say.
4. No matter how lofty your ideas may be or sound, let the boss's opinion overrule.
5. Never impose your ideas on the boss; he has the right to accept or reject it. If he does accept it, he is right; and if he rejects it, he is also right.

Your boss is always the boss and you are always the subordinate.

Rule 8

KEEP YOUR COOL WHEN AROUND THE BOSS

The boss never needs your tantrums. Learn to keep your cool when around him. No matter your emotional hangover, drop all your baggage at the doorstep; the boss doesn't need any of it, neither do your colleagues.

You must also learn to take some nonsense from the boss without losing your cool. Some bosses are friendly; but some others could be nasty. For the nasty ones, while it may just be a mood thing for some, others are simply incorrigible and impossible. It's your duty to learn to take them in whichever package they come.

The boss with a bad attitude knows that he has gotten one. Who knows whether it was that same attitude that took him to the top? In any case, while at the top, he is the boss and with that attitude he can aggravate you and stop your beautiful career.

You must know how to separate your ego and anger from the passions and emotions of your job. Don't allow your anger and ego to get in the way of your job. Your boss does not need any of your ego, anger and tantrums. All he needs is your self-esteem and your cool.

You may have observed that, during interviews, people are often asked if they can work under pressure. Pressure always produces tension. Tension, when not properly handled and managed, can push you to your breaking point or make you lose your mind.

Never give in to pressure! Manage your pressure and keep your cool, no matter the negative attitude of the boss! Always remember that you can do two important things with your emotions: **you can allow your emotion to lead you to demotion or you can allow it to lead you to promotion.** How you respond to issues and provocations will determine where you end up.

You have emotional freedom when your emotion works in your favor. With emotional calmness, you achieve a win-win outcome in your dealings. So, if you are going to make the best of your career and get promoted fast, don't forget to see yourself as a partner with your boss. See your emotional discharge as a way to either ruin or build up your business.

Therefore, don't keep malice with your boss; don't be bitter towards him. Your negative emotions may be showing on your countenance. In that case, you would be indirectly telling him, "I am not pleased with your authority over me." And with that, he will also be looking for a way to dislodge you quickly. Thus, always stay calm when around the boss.

Take control of your emotions. Discipline yourself not to express negative emotions when they arise (and they will surely do). Refuse to express your negative emotions when around the boss. Anger destroys and ruins quickly than any other negative emotion. To give it power over you will make you a fool. As Solomon, the wisest king in his generation said, "**Anger rests in the bosom of a fool**" (Ecclesiastes 7:9).

Rule 9

TURN HIS FOOLISHNESS INTO FULLNESS OF BLESSING

Have you ever heard the story of the Patriarch of the Christian faith, by the name of Noah? This man was so godly in his generation that he found favor in the sight of the Almighty God. God decided to spare him and save him from His wrath in his generation.

This man was also able to get his three sons saved from the destruction of God through the flood. The children were saved, not because they were so special or had found any favor from God, but because of their father.

Do you know that you also have your job because of your boss?

The story of Noah in the Bible further has it that, some day after the flood, he was drunk and got naked.

One of his sons saw his nakedness and left him in that condition to call his brothers to come and see their father's foolishness. But these other siblings were wiser. Instead of coming to see their father's foolishness and make it the talk of the town, they covered him up.

When their father woke up from his wine, he knew what happened - **the boss always knows!** Noah knew what his younger son had done; so he cursed him and blessed the others.

How do you handle your boss's foolishness? Do you go about making jest of him? Do you spread the news of his foolishness? Do you engage your other colleagues to discuss this?

The truth is that, no matter how much you try to destroy the boss and make fun of his foolishness, there will always be one among your colleagues who will be loyal to the boss and who will always report your acts to the boss.

So, **if you are going to get promoted fast, always learn to turn your boss's mistakes, and foolishness into fullness of blessing for yourself.** Be kind enough to correct and cover his mistakes. Stand in for him where you can - administratively, emotionally or in decision making. The boss will always be happy when you tend to cover and correct his error in private, without you spreading the news of his mistakes, errors and foolishness.

28

Rule 10

AVOID RELATIONSHIP ENTROPY WITH YOUR BOSS

Relationship entropy is when your relationship is running out of energy.

There is always a natural tendency in all working relationship to move towards entropy. Have you ever been irritated at the sight of your boss or the sound of his voice? Have you ever wished your boss was out of the office, either on a long vacation, annual leave, or some long distance corporate executive meetings?

If you have ever had this kind of feeling or thought whenever you think about your boss, your relationship with your job and the boss is running towards entropy.

Relationship entropy does not just happen; it is caused by unresolved issues that have resulted in emotional bottlenecks, administrative anger and career jeopardy. Normally, you may see some of the reactions as attacks on your person, which might make you want to become nasty towards the boss; or make you resist him, take him for granted and eventually badmouthing him.

If you are going to get promoted fast, avoid relationship entropy with the boss. **All relationships are a function of the time invested in them.** You can only increase the value of a relationship by investing more time in it. Take time to talk to your boss when his energy level seems high. Ask questions to know his pains and how you can help turn them into gains.

Never allow pressures of feelings to turn you into a recluse, so much that you are avoiding the boss. He knows when you like him and when you don't. And the truth is that neither of the two dispositions has much impact on the boss; your love or hatred has little to do with him, but a lot to do with you.

So, stay connected to your boss. Avoid relationship entropy and your promotion will come fast.

Rule 11

DOUBLE YOUR BOSS'S NET WORTH

The boss does not like deficit. So, he will naturally dislike employees that will always make him lose profit or expose him to bankruptcy. You owe the boss and yourself the duty to ensure that the company is making more profit and not losses.

If you are going to double your boss's net worth, then you have to increase your own productivity and that of all those that matter to the organization and business growth.

Always ask how you can increase sales and double the company's net worth. Once the boss realizes that you are always thinking in terms of the general profit of himself and the company, and not only about your own salary and profit, he will definitely promote you above all others.

It is the nature of an average man to think in terms

of his personal success, but **the excellent and ever growing person thinks in terms of the success of all around him.** So, the excellent employee will always think of doubling the net worth of his boss, his colleagues, and his organization first. When you think like this, even your colleagues will fight for your promotion because you always think ahead and are mindful of the security of their jobs.

Rule 12

BE PARTICULAR ABOUT WHAT THE BOSS IS PARTICULAR ABOUT

What does your boss like to talk about? What excites him? What makes him happy? What infuriates him?

What is your boss's other passion in life, apart from his work? Does he like football? Does he talk about his wife or children more? Is he a religious freak, or an approval-loving person? What excites him? Is it meeting people, staying alone, traveling?

Discover the flow of your boss and go with him.

When the boss realizes that you always like to get along with his flow, he will be very comfortable with you. He will tell you things he likes to do. You will become his secret and unofficial confidant - because you understand his flow and you are more particular about whatever he is particular about.

The reason many don't get the boss's favor, blessings and promotion is because they are more particular about their own things than those of the boss! So, when the boss is discussing issues of interest to him with them, they always want to change the topic to their own areas of interest or need.

When the boss realizes that you are too self-centered, he can never entrust you with his business, for you will do damage to his business by enriching yourself alone.

To receive the boss's favor and promotion, do the following:

1. Learn the greatest pains and frustrations of your boss and eliminate at least one of them.

2. See that problems get resolved before they reach the boss's desk. If you must present the boss a present problem, also go armed with the solution.

3. Keep the boss informed. Neither let good news nor bad news come from anyone but you.

Don't discuss the boss with others; they are likely to spill the beans on you.

Rule 13

OBTAIN KNOWLEDGE TO IMPROVE YOUR OUTPUT

Never stop learning.

Have you ever heard the saying, "a wise man is strong: yes, a man of knowledge increases strength" (Proverbs 24:5)?

Every instructional information and knowledge you gather about your career makes you a better person and improves your chances of promotion faster on your job. If you want your boss to like you and keep giving you a raise and a promotion, you have to study and read by yourself.

You must have what 1 call "self-made improvement and training seminars" all alone. You have to read books, journals and other informative publications. Get information from the Internet and other sources on better ways or more efficient approaches and techniques for doing your job in the 21st century. This can increase not just your output, but that of the entire corporation and your boss.

Review leading books on your professional field. Consult reference materials. There is no career on earth that a book has not been written about or that a new publication or article has not just been released about. By reading and adding information to your database, you are doing yourself a great deal of good, and very soon, your boss will notice your intellectual upgrade and definitely get you a raise and a promotion.

Never be lazy about adding information and knowledge to your life. Solomon, the great king said, "For a soul to be without knowledge is not good" (Proverbs 19:2). He also said, "Wise man lay up knowledge" (Proverbs 10:14).

So, get information that is relevant to your job.
Let it be detailed and concise for all to understand quickly, especially the boss.
Let it be accurate.
Let it be timely.
Let it address current issues and show the way forward.

Always remember that there is no knowledge that is wasted. What you learn and know today may be useful tomorrow. Keep on learning; read to refill your wells of inspiration and performance.

Rule 14

SEE WHAT THE BOSS DOESN'T SEE, DO WHAT HE CAN'T DO AND GIVE ALL THE CREDIT TO HIM

There is no one that is perfect or that knows it all. As good as the boss is; as sound, intelligent and powerful as he may be, there are certain things he is bound to miss out in the course of the job.

Has your boss ever mistakenly missed the balancing of the sheets? Has he ever forgotten to close the deal properly, without leaving some loopholes? Has he ever forgotten to "cross the t's" and dot the i's"?

Yea! Sometimes the boss makes mistakes that might be little but very grievous to his own self and the general corporation. You owe him the duty to watch his back, correct his mistakes, see what he doesn't see, do what he cannot do; and when all is done right, give all the credit to him. When the boss is sure you are not willing to take the credit, he gives you all the credit and he himself spreads your testimonials around.

The boss doesn't like those who will expose his frailties; he hired you to complement him and not to contend with him. Honor the boss, protect him from his own errors and correct him politely. He will love you for it and surely promote you.

Rule 15

NEVER UNDERMINE THE BOSS'S SPOUSE

Every boss is particular about his wife or her husband. **If you want to see a boss's unpleasant side, then despise what he or she highly esteems.**

If you want the boss' favor and promotion fast, learn the habit of treating his spouse with ultimate regard, respect and honor. I mean genuine respect, and not flatteries. Genuineness is easily detected, so also is flattery.

When you treat a man's spouse and family with genuine honor and respect, they automatically make recommendations regarding your promotion. How? They are part of the invisible and unofficial committee members that determine who is next in line for promotion.

Many have lost their promotion because they have deliberately undermined their boss's spouse and family. It is a natural disaster for you to try to treat your boss's spouse and family members in a negative way. When you show respect for your boss's spouse, it could influence your boss on the day of decision taking concerning your promotion.

There is no man or woman who is not being influenced, partly or fully, by a spouse, a family member, or even a mistress. In fact, sometimes a mistress is much more influential than the spouse! So, be very careful. Whenever a decision to promote someone is being taken, one way or the other, the boss is influenced by someone close to his heart.

Never forget that you are on your job for success and promotion. And one of the easiest ways to accomplish that is by treating your boss's spouse right. **Your boss's spouse has the power to influence your stay, promotion, demotion and termination on your job!**

Rule 16

NEVER BE AN ONLOOKER, BE A STAKEHOLDER

The problem with many employees is that when coming on their job or into an organization, they have a lackadaisical attitude towards corporate progress. They are more of "what is in it for me?" than "what can I put in it to make it great for all?"

Nothing kills the chances of a promotion faster than the "onlooker" attitude. It is the attitude of the small-minded and a lazy person. If you have that attitude, your boss knows and you can be sure there will be no positive appraisal for you, not to talk of a promotion.

See, the boss is watching you. Whether you know it or not, there is an invisible spy that is reporting on you. In any case, most times you are also reporting yourself - your nonchalant attitude, your sloppiness and your side comments of "is it my job?" Am I supposed to do that?" and "It is none of my business" are all being noted. Every of such comments will definitely put a minus on your appraisal. And you can be sure that you are on your way out.

The boss loves and promotes only the man who takes the boss's business as his. He only promotes a man who has, in his sub-conscious mind, made himself or herself a voluntary shareholder and a stakeholder. An employee with a shareholder and a stakeholder mentality does his job as if he owns the business. He does not care about who gets the credit; what matters to him is that the business must never suffer loss, and there must be an ever increasing profiting. So, he is not stopping at anything! He does his own work well and minds other people's business in the interest of the company. The boss can never deny this man his promotion.

I have done things that were not naturally in my jurisdiction to do because they were not part of my work, but I never saw things that way. Once I knew that something would be good and would improve my boss's life and his work, I did it and it has opened doors of unusual opportunities and promotion for me.

Don't just sit down and look, participate and be a stakeholder!

Rule 17

KNOW YOUR BOSS'S VISION AND SPEAK HIS BUSINESS LANGUAGE

Every organization has a driving vision and mission. Every boss has a vision and a mission. **Not knowing your boss's vision and business language is like being on a vehicle without knowing the destination.**

Take time to know your boss's vision. What is he trying to do on this job or in this business? Who is he trying to reach and is he reaching them the right way? Then ask yourself: Are you helping him to reach them the right way? Are you helping him to reach his destination with your job performance and attitude? If not, what can you do to change and bring a proper focus on your direction?

The boss will know when you know and understand his vision and also speak his business language. Every

43

business and organization has its culture and language.

To show that you are on your job with an overriding passion for the success of your job, career and your boss, catch his vision, know his mission and speak his business language. Many are not promoted, not because they don't do their job well, but because they don't know the vision of the house in which they are working. They cannot speak their boss's business language. They don't even care to know the specific terminologies relating to their job. Yet, the truth is that these seemingly little things determine whether you get promoted or not.

Rule 18

NEVER TAKE ADVANTAGE OF YOUR BOSS

Sometimes the boss can be nice to a few people. These are counted as the few privileged ones. They know intimate things about the boss; they are privy to certain information from the boss. They can get down on one-on-one and heart-to-heart discussions with the boss.

If you are one of such few privileged few, never try to take advantage of your boss. Learn to treat him with utmost respect! **Learn to separate your friendship with your boss from your commitment to your job.** Learn to place the boss as the boss at any time, but especially when colleagues, visitors and guests are around.

No matter how much the boss confides in you and lets you in on some private matter, whether concerning his life or the business, never share it with others. Keep it to yourself! You will love yourself and the boss will appreciate you for it.

Also, don't forget that certain people will come on the job after you, and based on their experience and professionalism, they may enjoy some perks more than you who have been on the job and also close to the boss. Please, never take it out on the boss, and don't see it as an opportunity to override the boss or ask for unnecessary raise for yourself! When you do, the boss will see you as a threat and a usurper, who takes advantage of special relationships. This display of gross immaturity may cost you your job and your relationship.

Do you know anything special and confidential about your boss? Keep it to yourself!

Do you know anything about his intimate relationships or associations? Keep it to yourself.

Don't ever spill it or try to use it against him, even when you two have a misunderstanding. If you do, someone will show you the door.

A king once had a forbidden sexual affair with a woman; and his servant, who happened to be his confidant, witnessed the incident. So, he started misbehaving, and whenever the king wanted to deal with him, he reminded him of his illicit act. So the king was in bondage to him.

One day the king decided he was going to be free from this bondage. He sent for all his chiefs and other subordinates and started a funny story about the stupidity of promiscuity. He started sharing stories of his escapades and, in doing so, mentioned the forbidden affair he had and how much he regretted it.

When the people heard the king's story, they simply laughed at his escapades and also appreciated his openness with them. At this point, the servant who had always blackmailed the king was shocked that the king had exposed himself, so to expose him was not possible anymore, for there was nothing else to expose!

Then the king called the disloyal servant and denounced him in the presence of all. He lost his position.

Never take advantage of the boss because he can always find his way around issues!

Rule 19

BE CAUTIOUS AND ETHICAL AROUND THE BOSS

The boss, no matter how irrational, unrefined or deficient he might be, is still the boss, even when he is without his underwear. In other words, no matter the condition in which you may find your boss, you must always have it in your conscious and sub-conscious mind that he must always be treated with the greatest decorum and etiquette.

In the business world or any organization, those who do not follow the rules of accepted behavior lose. It is simple as that. One major aspect of etiquette is demeanor! **What you say and how you say it, as well as how you act, in a professional setting is very important**. In its simplest form, demeanor can include things like positive and negative attitudes.

People react more favorably to individuals who

have good posture and demeanor. So, when you are around the boss, certain behaviors and ethical standards are expected of you. For instance, when around the boss, a gentle smile and not a high goofy guffaw, is expected of you. A calm smile exudes dignity and power, and is sure to be relaxing for you and even your boss.

Aside from this, other forms of behavior expected of you when around the boss include being always cautious of how you respond when he calls you, as well as how you sit when around him. Your posture conveys a great deal about who you are and your view of the boss, his business and his success.

So, when with the boss:

Never take a seat, without him asking you to sit.

Learn to always respond with "yes, sir", or "yes, madam".

Learn to use the words "please", "sorry" and "thank you".

Stand up when your boss introduces you.

Never laugh too wildly around the boss.

Always be behind the boss when both are walking the stairs.

Always get the door while making an entrance with

the boss.

Always take the front seat while riding with the boss, except he asks you to ride with him in the back seat of the car.

Learn to shake the boss firmly with a smile when he gives you a hand.

Never use slangs or jargons around the boss; choose your words.

When having a meeting and you are privileged to be sitting next to the boss, kindly pull out his or her seat. Never sit, until the boss is seated and let him ask you to take your seat before you do.

When the boss gives you a gift, accept it and express your gratitude with expressions lie, "Thank you, boss" and "You are the best boss I've ever had." Most times, a boss never expects a gift in return.

A boss is always happy and comfortable around a very cautious, gentlemanly or ladylike employee. He watches you and knows you are a good ambassador of his company, business or organization. With this, he will never hesitate on your promotion and further training.

Rule 20

PRACTICE THE "PLATINUM RULE" WITH THE BOSS

There are bosses who don't care how things get done; all they want is for you to just get them done, and done right. However, there are others who care how you get things done, and they want it done their way.

Once you have a boss you need to practice and apply the Platinum Rule. The Platinum Rule is the sequel to the "Golden Rule." The Golden Rule states that "Do unto others what you want done to you, or treat others the way you wish to be treated." But the Platinum Rule differs. It states that "Treat others the way they want to be treated."

The problem is that most employees don't know how the boss wants to be treated; so they treat the boss the way they would like to be treated. But that would not work in the 21st century business and corporate world. Every boss has his own peculiarity and how he would like to be treated. Some bosses don't mind you calling them by their first name. Some don't mind a light atmosphere around, while others are the serious minded type.

Your duty is to know your boss, which I will also talk about in a later rule. But knowing your boss is not enough if you want to get promoted fast; you must know your boss and treat him the way he would like to be treated.

The Platinum Rule allows you to make your boss feel comfortable in your presence and to also treat you well.

Rule 21

ALWAYS MAKE THE BOSS NOTICE YOU

One of the greatest havocs you can do to yourself while on your job is to be evasive of the boss. This could be because of your perception of him as being too hard, being a taskmaster or one who does not allow you rest when he is around you.

The moment you always make yourself evasive and always unnoticeable by the boss, you are shooting yourself in the foot. You may never get any promotion or a raise. A good employee must develop a style of being noticed by the boss as one who is always happy to be on the job, even when he is not happy. You must also show yourself as one who is happy to see the boss around, even when you don't like his presence.

The boss is always the boss. Whether you like his presence or not, there is nothing you can do about his status; but there is a lot the boss can

do about your own status. You need him the most; he doesn't need you that much, since he can always find a replacement for you. But you can make him feel like he cannot survive in his position without you! All you need is to do things exceptionally, so that your presence and your work are noticed!

Determine to be tasteful, formal, civilized, sophisticated, elegant, cultured, refined, hardworking, caring and discerning around the boss.

These qualities make your presence felt and your absence noticed! If you want the boss to notice you quickly and promote you fast, do the following:

- Be the first to arrive at the office.

- Be the last to leave the office.

- Do your work on time and finish without too much error.

- Help some of your colleagues that lag behind in their tasks.

- Work extra hours without expecting a raise.

- Improve the net worth of the boss always and never ask for a favor in return.

- Never talk about how much the company owes you for all you have been doing for them.

- Always dress up rather than down; learn to be formal.

- Be neat, be smart, be trendy and always smell nice.

Rule 22

NEVER TELL THE BOSS HOW HARD YOU ARE WORKING

One of the stories in the Holy Bible that I find fascinating is the story of the prodigal son and his brother. The prodigal son is an example of a wasteful, lazy and fun-loving employee, who wants all the good things of life and the perks of the company, without paying the price of sacrifice and commitment.

The brother felt so bad, having been the one always helping their father on the job, getting the business running, bringing in turnovers in their millions and yet without any special raise, holiday or treats. After the return of his reckless brother, the father threw a party on the return of his lost son. When the older brother came back, he became angry with his father. He said, "How can I be this faithful, diligent, serving, and never asking for a raise and you never gave me special perks; and now this one who has squandered your money in reckless living came and you killed a calf and make merry?"

The father's response was amazing! He said, "Your brother was lost but now is found; but you are all that I have left. The new business acquisition and empire are all yours. In other words, it is a waste to set your eyes on the small perks of life and immediate gratification because what awaits you is that you are the next CEO of this company!"

Never tell the boss how hard you are working; he can see it. But even more important is that the invisible God Almighty can also see your patience, diligence and hard work and He will miraculously promote you beyond your imagination! You might be appointed and given special privileges and position as an executive director or the next manager or CEO of the corporation.

The boss is always watching, and he knows who is working hard and who also has his interest at heart.

Rule 23

BE TACTFUL IN FLAUNTING YOUR WEALTH AND POSSESSIONS AROUND YOUR BOSS

One of the quickest ways to get negative attention from some bosses is to try to do and be what they already are!

A boss will always want to be ahead of you. And he would want it to reflect in all he does. Therefore, it is wisdom for you to intentionally make him feel so. **It is good for you psychologically and for him.** Once he realizes that you always want what he wants, he would tend to see you as being in a direct psychological competition with him.

I have seen people lose their jobs and thrown into

sudden pain and penury because of their lack of self-restraint around their bosses. For instance, a friend lost his job, and according to him it was because he wore a shirt with the same label and price as that of the boss. When the boss noticed this, he thought, "This boy must be stealing from me" - because he knew the number of years it took him and what it cost him to get to that level before he could afford that shirt.

The truth however is that my friend had a second stream of income that helped him afford that shirt. But the boss never knew; so, he sacked him.

Another friend told me of how he lost his job because he was driving a car that was more expensive than his boss's. To add insult to injury, he was also traveling on the same air class with the boss. Some bosses aren't very comfortable with such.

So, do yourself a favor; make the boss always feel he is the boss at all levels. Let him think you are truly his subordinate. The boss is in a class all by himself.

Rule 24

BEFRIEND YOUR BOSS AND NEVER DESPISE THE FRIENDSHIP WITH HIM

The greatest stupidity of any employee is to despise the friendship of his or her boss. The fact that the boss has chosen you to be a special friend with a special privilege and rapport with him should not be seen as a license to disrespect him. If you are going to be successful and get promoted fast, learn to befriend your boss and never abuse the friendship.

No matter the level of closeness and friendship with your boss, always draw the limit in your conscious and sub-conscious mind that "this is my boss and no matter the friendship he must be treated as such."

Never try to talk to the boss who is your friend in a casual manner before your colleagues. Never try to touch the boss in a manner that is unbecoming of office and business etiquette because you are friends. Never yell back at the boss because you are a special friend. Never refuse instructions from the boss because you are friends. Most importantly, know when the boss is not in the mood for friendly boss relationship.

Learn how to switch between friend-boss relationship and subordinate-boss relationship.

Never discuss your friendship with the boss in a despising manner with colleagues.

Never take advantage of your friendship with the boss as a means of breaking office and business rules.

Rule 25

PRACTICE THE GOLDEN RULE WITH THE BOSS

The Golden Rule states, "Do unto others what you want done unto you." This rule is about you putting yourself in the shoes of the boss. It's about viewing yourself one day as the boss, and asking yourself how you would like to be treated by your staff.

Most people like to be honored. They like to receive special respect and be highly revered as the boss! If that is your thought of yourself when you become the boss, then do the same thing to your boss!

Try to make a list of "How I wish to be treated as the boss." Most lists would read like these:

- I would like to be respected by all staff.

- At my appearance in the office in the morning, I would like my staff to acknowledge my presence.

- I would like my staff to stand straight and talk to me when addressing an issue.

- I would like my staff to smile at my appearance, and also smile when I correct them.

- I would like my staff never to argue with me in the presence of their colleagues, guest or customer.

- Sometimes, I would like my staff to make me feel I am the best and that they owe me their allegiance on the job.

The list goes on and on! So whatever that is good, pure, true, lovely, and of honest report that you can think of if you are the boss, go ahead and do the same for your boss and you will be promoted fast!

Rule 26

NEVER FIGHT YOUR BOSS

Ever heard, "You can never win a fight with the boss"? No matter your level of intelligence, creativity, excellence, productivity and indispensability on your job, never allow it to get into your head and push you to the point of fighting your boss.

No matter what you do, who you think you are, and what you think you know, you can never win a fight with the boss. The boss pays your salary. He hired you for his interest and for the general benefit of the corporation. So, **if you are going to survive, never fight the boss.** Your promotion is in your ability to always stay calm with the boss. Fighting the boss is a fight you cannot win under any circumstance; so never bother to do it.

Always realize that in every organization, business enterprise or conglomerate, there will be disagreement and debates. **Disagreements and debates are healthy occurrences that help organizations move forward, provided there are no personal or selfish interests.**

Accept that you will have many debates with your boss during your career. Debate all you want, but never allow it to escalate to a fight because this is your wisdom and guarantee to success and promotions.

To avoid a fight with your boss:

- Never allow your anger to control you.
- Learn to compromise quickly or align yourself with the boss's decision.
- Make your points but accept the boss's final decision.
- Never try to force your opinion on the boss, even if the opinion is right and the boss is not willing to take or implement it for now.
- Learn how to run away from a fight today; tomorrow you might be the boss.
- Know your boss's emotional elasticity. The boss can "snap" also.
- Never yell back at the boss! Never!

Follow these principles and you become a sure candidate for promotion.

Rule 27

KNOW YOUR BOSS

Bosses come in different packages, contents and wraps. To be successful on your job, career or organization, you must know your boss - who he is, and what he wants and what moves him into action.

Every boss is unique and responds differently to the situations of life, work, family and social issues. **Know your boss and treat him based on your discovery of who he is.** Discern the kind of person your boss is. Is he an informal person when you have to give him information or communicate with him? Or is he a formal person, who does like you to write out detailed information, ideas and proposal by e-mail, letter or a combination of both?

My boss was not a formal person. He liked verbal communication of ideas; and I must be simple and concise when relating my ideas and information to him. The discovery of your boss makes your work easier and also helps you to treat him the way he likes to be treated. So, learn how to gather knowledge about your boss and make him comfortable. To also make him comfortable, ask questions.

Please, note:

- Ask for an up-to-date job description from your boss.
- Spend time in your boss's presence.
- Pay attention to the way he likes his things done and do them that way.
- Make your discovery about your boss of utmost importance.
- Study your boss. Watch his move and know his pattern.
- Ask questions on what he wants you to do and how to do it.
- Relate with your boss's spouse and get to know one or two things about your boss's working ideology. Often, bosses talk or complain about their staff to their spouse directly or indirectly.

Rule 28

SMILE AT THE BOSS EVEN WHEN YOU DON'T LIKE HIM OR WHAT HE IS SAYING!

The boss is the chief instructor or corrector of staff members in an organization. Some bosses may be polite in correcting you and treating you like an adult; while others may be brash, inconsiderate, rude and treat you like an immature or stupid nonentity.

Whichever way your boss treats you, talks to you or corrects you, never frown or express anger at what he is saying. Be careful and just keep calm. Give a smile, be quick to say sorry no matter what your ego says.

A smile is infectious. It is a powerful force. It can stop and break the most hardened and difficult person. The workplace can be a very tough terrain, with a lot of pressure, difficulties, challenges and tasks.

Sometimes this can make the boss edgy and likewise your colleagues. A smile around the boss helps reduce the tension and pressure. You see, you don't have to like the boss before you give him a smile. You smile at him because he is the boss and, in one moment, he can determine the course of your career!

Never forget that smiling and laughing have a place inside all companies. People notice and respect those who are confident and in control. Happy people are people who are in control.

Never forget that the smallest things always count, and the easiest thing in the world is to produce a smile. The boss will always remember you - if not for anything; at least, for the smile you always give, both in pleasant situations and unpleasant ones. This forms part of your unseen C.V. for promotion.

Rule 29

NEVER COME TO WORK WITH THE BOSS WITH YOUR EMOTIONAL GARBAGE

Have you ever seen any man or woman without an issue in this life? No! None at all. We all have issues – family issues, financial issues, marital issues, accommodation issues, business issues, emotional issues, and so on. If care is not taken, all these issues have a way of affecting our actions and reactions at the workplace.

However, **as you come to work with the boss, you must learn to drop your issues at home**. Learn to separate your issues from your work. The boss does not need any of your issues; all he wants is your top performance.

When you walk through the entrance of the door to your office, forget about your issues; concentrate on

70

giving the boss your best shot! You must be focused. When you allow your issues, they will distract you and give your colleagues an advantage over you.

Learn to simplify your life, never let your issues affect your expression and performance. Doing so has a way of making the boss to dislike you, and see you as one who is always crying wolf when there is none.

No matter what, keep the boss out of your issues because he has enough on his hands already; only let him in on your issues when he asks what's up!

Once you are able to separate your issues and emotional baggage from your work, you will be seen as one who can work under pressure and adverse conditions without supervision, and thus deserving a promotion.

Rule 30

ALWAYS REMEMBER YOUR OFFICE ETIQUETTE

Every organization spends so much money on training, improving and educating staff on proper office etiquette and guidelines for successful customer and work relations.

It is important that you always remember and keep this business etiquette in your view; it is part of what forms your condition and consideration for promotion. Remember that the boss is always watching; so, practice it around the boss, customers and colleagues.

You can always meet the expectations of the boss on office etiquette by doing the following:

- Return phone calls within twenty-four hours. Never forget to ask if it is a good time for the individual to talk.

- When around the boss, keep your phones on silent, or vibration. Learn to withhold incoming calls when talking with the boss.

- Take permission from the boss before taking your important calls.

- Never keep the boss waiting on the line without an explanation or sincere apology.

- Answer e-mails that are urgent immediately, and those that require additional information within two days or maximum of one week.

- Never be late for any meeting with the boss.

- Be in the office or meeting venue before the boss. It is not right for the boss to be waiting for you; it is better for you to be waiting for the boss.

- Never exceed your allotted time during a presentation.

- Address your boss with the proper title.

- Learn all you can about table manners.

- Be quick to say "thank you, sir/ma"; "I am sorry, sir/ma"; "consider it done, sir/ma".

- When playing golf or any other game with the boss, never cheat!

When you keep your etiquette around the boss he will recommend you for a promotion.

'

Rule 31

BE LOYAL AND PROTECTIVE OF THE BOSS

The story of David and King Saul in the Bible is one of loyalty in the face of opposition, distrust, fear and persecution – which eventually culminated in a mighty promotion.

A staff is expected to be faithful and loyal to the boss, watching out for the interest of the boss, protecting the boss, and defending his coast and territories from intruders, fifth columnists and destroyers.

Your action and words on your job and around your boss must depict loyalty. When you demonstrate loyalty to the boss, your promotion is guaranteed. You must avoid disloyalty completely.

Watch out for these signs of disloyalty in yourself against the boss:

- You become disloyal when you begin to operate with an *espirito indipendieto* attitude. That is, when you demonstrate an independent spirit against your boss's command. You are being disloyal and dangerous to the boss, and he may sack you.

- You are disloyal when you take offense easily against the boss's instruction.

- You are disloyal when you do your own thing without the boss's approval.

- You are disloyal when you become passive about the boss's instructions; it is a sign that you don't like the boss and you are losing interest in the job; you can never bring increase.

- You are disloyal when you become critical of everything about the boss.

- You are disloyal when you become deceptive. The boss can identify this act of disloyalty!

Practice the following acts of loyalty and the boss will promote you:

- Talk favorably about your boss.

- Celebrate your boss's speeches.

- Never encourage complaints against the boss.

- Be punctual at work.

- Be happy with your boss.

- Make sure all is well with the boss.

- Never divert your boss's customers and clients.
- Always take notes when the boss is talking to you.
- Learn to give gifts to your boss.
- Be content with your boss and yourself as his assistance.
- Accept your boss's leadership gladly.

NEVER TAKE ANYTHING FROM THE BOSS WITHOUT HIS PERMISSION

Familiarity, as they say, always has the tendency of bringing contempt. But such contempt mostly comes from the unwise and the unknowledgeable. The boss's friendship or kindness towards you must never become a thing of regret to him.

I have seen people abusing the special privileges they have with the boss by doing things that are unlawful and unethical around him. Don't forget that the boss is always watching your attitude. He is studying your character and disposition, and he does not like it when you try to abuse his friendliness.

One of the ways you can displease the boss is for you to take his things without his permission. Never do this. **Taking things from the boss without his permission is a direct insult and slap on his face.** Taking things from the boss without his permission is dishonoring him and making him your equal.

- Never take things from the boss without his permission.
- Never take his pen without his permission.
- Never enter his office without his permission.
- Never take anything from his bag, drawers or closet without his permission.
- Never take any drink, food or fruits from the boss's refrigerator without his permission.
- Never use the boss's car without his permission.
- Never use the boss's drivers without his permission.
- Never try the boss's stuff without his permission.

When you give the boss his rightful place, the boss will also place you in your right place. Promotion!

Rule 33

NEVER REJECT THE BOSS'S DIRECTIVES

There was once a man in my country who served in one of the most powerful commissions. This commission dealt with corrupt leaders and people in the society. This man was powerful and untouchable, while in this commission; however, before being made the head of the commission, he had been drafted from another commission, where he had been a subordinate to someone.

On assuming his new position, he flagrantly despised authorities, including his former superiors, because he was powerful and had the backing of the government of the day. By doing this, he failed to remember that the boss is always the boss.

No matter how much power, influence and control you wield around yourself, once you have a boss or superior, you must control yourself. Obey instructions and remember that the boss is always the boss.

Unfortunately for the man I was telling you about, the tenure of the government that had empowered him soon ended, and another government took over. The new government redeployed the man to where he originally was. The double promotion granted him by the previous government had been reversed! But not only was he demoted, the incumbent government further humiliated him by eventually dismissing him.

What were his offences?

- Flagrant refusal to obey the order and directives of the boss to report in his office.
- Dressing improperly (in plain clothes) while on official courtesy visit to the president with other senior executives of the commission.
- Instituting legal action against the commission.
- Refusal to go to his new posting location.
- Instituting legal action against the boss while still a serving officer.
- Instituting legal action against his nation at an international court
- All of these allegations sprang from flagrant disobedience to authority.
- Never refuse the boss's instructions.

Rule 34

WARN THE BOSS POLITELY

Mistakes, errors, and misjudgments are part of our lives as humans. Nobody is above this frailty. Every mortal, be it the boss or the subordinate, is imperfect. Simply put, we all make mistakes – and that includes the boss.

It is the duty of the subordinate to forewarn the boss, correct him and guide him in the face of errors, mistakes and misjudgments which he might not realize. However, the issue here is not just the errors and mistakes of the boss but how you correct or forewarn him.

People do not care how much you know until they know how much you care.

The boss wants you to protect his interest, watch his back and keep him from errors and fatal mistakes that can jeopardize his life and business. But he is also careful on how you warn him. He wants to protect his own honor and privileges. So, whenever the boss is wrong, find a discreet way of correcting his wrong and warning him of the danger and consequences of any wrong moves and decisions.

To warn the boss, do the following:

- Get the facts of the matter and analyze it properly before correcting or warning the boss about it.

- Never correct or warn the boss in the open.

- Where wrong statements and utterances are involved, if you have the opportunity to talk after the boss, do justice to his wrong statements.

- Walk up to the boss in the private and show him he is wrong and warn him of consequences.

- Determine the right atmosphere before making the move for correction.

- Don't make his correction an object of discussion and mockery among colleagues.

- Always make the boss realize that you have always known him to be a great boss, and you will never allow any mistake to taint his greatness, therefore, you have chosen to help.

Rule 35

ALWAYS REMEMBER YOU ARE ASSIGNED TO DO THE WILL OF THE BOSS

The phrase, "Thy will be done", was popularized by Jesus Christ, our Lord and Master. He was in a situation where He needed to choose between what pleased Him and what pleased His Father and Master, God Almighty!

Jesus Christ had every right and power to do what was pleasing, convenient and satisfying to Him, but He did not. He was conscious of the fact that the position in which He was standing on earth then, was not by His own making or power; He realized He had his standing because His boss gave Him the right to go and occupy that office where He stood. In other words, He was sent. Therefore, doing anything against the will of the Father would be nothing but rebellion, disloyalty and insubordination.

You are assigned to your boss to carry out his instructions. **Never do anything your own way which is not the way of the boss**; do it the way of the boss.

You are assigned to the boss and not to yourself! Your assignment is always to enable your boss succeed in some areas of his business and life. Never complicate issues for the boss, because you do not know why you are assigned to him. Where instructions are complicated, politely request for a clarification or written instruction.

Always remember that you are assigned to do the will of the boss.

Rule 36

PREPARE TO MEET THY BOSS

Preparation is said to be the mother of all great successes. Preparation is not what you do in the open; it is what you do in the closet, where no one sees you! **Preparation is who you are and what you do to get what you want in the open.**

If you want the boss to favor and promote you fast, then you have to learn the art of preparing to meet your boss. Never go into the presence of the boss without ready-made answers to likely questions, problems, challenges and difficulties that might arise on the job.

The boss wants answers and solutions, not more problems.

So, before you see the boss on any assignment, project or forthcoming ideas, do the following:

- Get your mind ready and prepared with the right attitude towards your work and the boss.

- Where you need to make presentations, rehearse and refine your delivery.

- Gather all information on your subject of discussion with the boss, don't appear confused and lost on your subject.

- Practice the habit of effective communication and simplicity of language.

- Before a meeting, prepare yourself thoroughly. This could be through a written note to collate your thoughts so that you do not shoot off the target.

- Where possible, get a back-up for your important information.

- When you are meeting the boss, dress and smell properly. Your appearance determines the amount of audience the boss will give you. Review your notes before stepping before the boss.

Always remember that your preparation speaks louder than your words when it comes to how much you love what you are going to do and whom you are to meet. You never appear before a governor or president without preparing to meet him. Do likewise to your boss.

Rule 37

DRESS FOR THE JOB, AND DRESS FOR THE BOSS

How you dress says a lot about you. Your clothes can affect you, your mood, your spirit and the flow you have on your job and the flow of your boss to you. When you dress in a sloppy or shabby manner, you are sending a wrong a signal to your boss. In fact, what you are saying is:

- I don't like this job
- I don't like my boss and am not excited about his person
- I wish I could get out of this job.

The way you dress speaks for you - whether you need to be encouraged, improved or promoted. There are certain things you must keep in mind about your appearance, if you desire promotion in your workplace. These include:

- Look at how those in the position to which you aspire are dressed and groomed, and then follow their leads.

- Dress appropriately and don't be overdressed! Pick the right colors for the office. Dress prudently.

- Always remember that your appearance influences your emotions.

- Your appearance sends a message to others, either to honor and promote you, or dishonor and demote you.

- Your clothing educates others on how you desire to be approached.

- Your clothing influences how others feel about you.

- Your appearance creates a climate of acceptance or rejection for you.

- Here are some basic rules of dressing for the job and the boss:

- Let your clothes be clean, well-fitting and in good condition.

- Keep your hair and nail tidy.

- Brush your mouth before going to bed and in the morning; keep fresh breath.

- Use perfumes and colognes sparingly, and especially if you have a strong body odor.

- Be well shaven.
- Nobody rejects a clean-looking man or woman; even the boss cannot reject you.

Rule 38

DON'T ALWAYS GET SICK

Some people are in the habit of falling sick weekly or bi-weekly! **Lazy people hide under the guise of sick leave, in order to evade work and responsibility.** Sickness is not a good thing and anybody can fall sick at any time. But never use sickness as an excuse for evading your work!

Does your wife get sick weekly and you have taken permission?

Do your kids fall sick regularly and you need to go on leave? Never indulge in this.

Don't play games with the boss; he knows when you are sick and when you are evading your job! Those who are always sick don't get promoted on the job.

Don't always use sickness as an excuse and avenue

for skipping your job. Learn how to stay healthy! **The healthier you are, the longer you can stay on your job and get promoted fast!**

Rule 39

DON'T STEAL THE BOSS'S TIME AND DON'T WASTE TIME

When you do not report to the office at the appropriate time, you are stealing the boss's time.

When you use the office hour to do your own job, you are stealing the boss's time.

When you are dilly-dallying during office hours, you are stealing the boss's time.

When you are sleeping at the wrong time during office hours, you are stealing the boss's time.

When you are busy loafing about, leaving your job and chatting with other people, you are stealing and wasting time.

When you always have one reason or the other for

not being in the office often, you are a time thief and a time waster.

The boss does not appreciate anyone who steals his time for his own private affairs. You are depleting him and denying him maximum benefit and the purpose of your earning.

Benjamin Franklin once said, "**Does thou love life? Then do not squander time, for that is the stuff life is made of.**"

Avoid time wasting. Delegate and do the following to maximize time:

- Be always on time for work.
- Create an atmosphere of "impossible distraction" for those who are calling for your attention but do not pay your salary.
- Avoid being distracted; if you can be distracted, you can be defeated.
- Stand up when unwanted visitors come, politely turn them down.
- Avoid clutters on your table.
- Review your responsibility.
- Never be absent from work without a serious and genuine reason.
- Give and spend your best time - and the boss will promote you.

Rule 40

NEVER DIVERT OR SCARE THE BOSS'S CUSTOMERS

If you want to be promoted by the boss, avoid sharp practices! These include diverting the boss's customers or scaring them so they can patronize your own private business or a friend's private business!

Every diversion of the boss's customer is a diversion of your own promotion and success. **Nature has retributions for negative practices.** When you indulge in sharp practices against your boss, you show disloyalty. It is wrong for you to be seen as a friend in the open, while behind the scenes, you become an enemy, impostor and a fifth columnist.

Your sharp practices will sooner or later give you away. You will be caught and fired without mercy.

Never forget that the boss's customers give you your livelihood and your salary. The transactions they do with the boss pay your monthly bill. Thus, encourage the boss's customers. In fact, drive more customers and clients to the boss, and you will end up with a promotion.

Rule 41

SERVE THE BOSS CUSTOMERS EXCEPTIONALLY

The difference between a thriving eatery and boutique is not the location, nor the price of their commodities; rather it is in how the customers are treated by the staff.

I once entered a popular eatery in Lagos, Nigeria at Isaac John Government Residential Area; as I drove into the parking lot, the security man was not friendly at all, his face was long drawn and he yelled at me even before I parked my car! I rolled down my car window and rebuked his naughtiness. Out of anger, I pulled out without entering the eatery; opposite this particular eatery was another eatery; as I pulled to the next eatery car park, the security man came rushing down with an umbrella, because it was raining!

He treated me like a special V.I.P.! He accorded me so much respect and salutations in the Sirs; as he ushered me to the entrance of the eatery. The second security man did the same, guiding me with a smile, I smiled back and tipped both security men after I had my meal. Then it occurred to me, that **how you treat your boss customers determine the profit your boss will make, and what will come to me.**

When you give a smile to a customer, you get a smile and a tip!

When you give, it does not come back to you in the same proportion, there is always a surplus! Always do your best to improve the bottom line of your company and your boss through a greater responsiveness to those who pay your salary.

Remember;

You are either servicing the customer or servicing someone who is servicing the customer.

Respond to customers exceptionally; meet their needs before they ask and solve their problems before they complain.

Give customers far more than they expect

Listen to complaining customers; solve their problems quickly, generously and happily.

Rule 42

PRACTICE POLITICS WITH THE BOSS WISELY

Politics is a normal occurrence at the workplace. **Everyone is involved in one politics or the other in life, but more especially in the corporate world.** The bigger the organization you work for, the more complex and more ferocious the politics is.

It is important to note that in every organization, there are people who will try to get ahead of you and they will play some politics around you to achieve their goal. Even the boss will play this politics with you. The boss sometimes will get involved in corporate or organizational politics. But he would likely need an alibi. And you might be his best alibi!

You must be careful how you play, so that you don't get

consumed in the organizational politics. But you must play - you cannot avoid it, no matter how reserved or sanctimonious you are!

While playing office politics, avoid discussing the boss with other co-workers. This will not work in your interest, as the boss always has his own eyes and ears among the staff.

Remember this: **Politics exists in your organization or corporation. You cannot bury your head and pretend it does not happen**; rather, study the players and set your own personal strategy of dealing with them wisely, as David did against his boss, King Saul in the Bible.

Rule 43

CAUSE NO DAMAGE TO THE BOSS

The boss is always particular about maximum profit, minimum risk and minimum loss. Always remember that any act that jeopardizes this could get you fired!

- Never allow those who are in competition with the boss cash in on valuable information or secrets from you.

- Never be careless with the company's information

- Never give room for theft or stealing from other colleagues to the detriment of the company and the boss.

- Avoid fire disaster that can claim your life or the boss's business.

- Never encourage activities of evil minds that

can bring the boss or the company to a ruin.

- Be careful when driving the company's car
- If you live in the staff quarters, take maximum care of it.
- Always report criminal activities.

Watch out for the boss's maximum profit. When you do this, your promotion is guaranteed.

Rule 44

NEVER EMBARRASS
THE BOSS

There are employees who never care whose ox is being gored. They believe they are people of truth and absolute truth. They do not believe in politeness or diplomacy. The truth must be told anyhow, even if it means the person involved is a superior.

Once you see yourself as a man who does not care about managing the truth with your boss, you will definitely not care about embarrassing him. This attitude will definitely get your finger burnt. **The rule of the game is that no matter how much truth you know, and no matter how right you are when dealing with the boss, you must be balanced in applying the truth.** Truth is a two-edged sword; it can either work for you or against you.

Never forget, the boss is your superior. Never talk to

him rudely, or embarrass him with your actions, no matter how right you are.

Constantly, display actions of honor toward the boss, such as:

- Standing up when talking to the boss.
- **Saying only positive things about him in the open, and saying the negative ones to him alone in the private.**
- Making the boss relax and comfortable always in your presence
- Never making the boss feel agitated at your presence because he cannot trust your comments or remarks!

Always make the boss leave your presence happy and grateful to God and humanity for knowing you and having you as one of his most valuable staff! When you learn to treat the boss right, the boss also treats your promotion fast!

Rule 45

KEEP A TO-DO LIST WHEN MEETING WITH THE BOSS

James M. Barrie said, "God gave us memory that we might have roses in December." Our memory is a powerful and extraordinary "computer", designed by God Almighty. Information and data in their billions are processed from the brain, precisely from the age of four to ninety or as long as we can live. But, most times, we find it difficult to remember everything that has been processed, because we are humans and we are limited by other matters. Simply put, sometimes memories do fail us!

So, when talking to the boss about your job and assignment, it is advisable to **keep a to-do notebook. This will help you to reduce the loss of instruction, information and directives!** Never forget that the boss wants the job done the way he says it to you.

For you to be on top of the job, whenever you are have an audience with the boss:

- Have a notepad and a good ball pen with you.
- Write down the boss's expectation of you.
- Ask the boss for an up-to-date description of your assignment.
- Ask questions about your job, and write down the boss's answers.
- Scribble down your doubts and clarify them before leaving the presence of the boss.

Rule 46

NEVER SNAP AT THE BOSS

For no reason are you permitted to yell back at the boss. No matter the situation, learn to keep your cool around the boss; he still holds the ace.

One day, I was in the office of a senior bank official of one of the old generation banks in my country, Nigeria. Here I was, seated as a customer in the bank with this senior official. At one point, an argument ensued between her and a junior staff. The staff lost control of her emotion and snapped back at her boss. Visibly furious, the boss instantly summoned another official and asked that the junior staff be issued a query, requesting her to give reasonable reasons why she must not be dealt with.

I believe that if the junior staff had kept her cool till after my departure, the boss might not have felt so slighted. That single indiscretion led to the flurry of disciplinary reactions from the boss.

Every time you snap, you lose your peace, joy and calmness. Anger rests in the bosom of a fool. Anger makes you snap. And you snap when you are stressed and the stress presents irritation, which results in a sharp emotional outburst. Do well to avoid this with the boss always.

As Lawrence J. Peter says, "**If you speak when you are angry, you will make the best speech you will ever regret.**"

Never snap at the boss!

Control your anger

Say to yourself, "I will not allow my anger to control me, I will control my anger!"

Once, the boss knows that, no matter what he says to you, you can keep your cool, you become the first candidate for consideration when the need for promotion arises!

Rule 47

NEVER FORCE YOURSELF ON THE BOSS

Have you ever seen people who like to have their way, no matter the resistance or the unwillingness of the other person? They push their way through, using all kinds of games and gimmicks, ranging from tears to name calling and blackmails.

Never be that kind of person to your boss. Learn to accept some no's from the boss and never try to force yourself on him. Don't blackmail him into seeing reason, or to implement your opinions, suggestions or desires.

Trying to force yourself on the boss will create another reputation for you. You will be seen as a traitor, a usurper and a *persona non grata*!

Never insist on your way with the boss.

Never force the boss into a corner to always do your will

Never make the boss give you certain jobs, positions or assignments, because of your relationship with him.

Learn to respect the boss's opinion

Learn to respect the boss's decisions and learn to accept the "no" from the boss.

Once the boss knows you are someone who never insists on his way, but rather do your best to consider all sides of a matter and follow his instructions, that will automatically qualify you for a promotion.

So, always avoid language that portrays you as forcing your way on the boss.

Rule 48

NEVER REPLY THE BOSS IN ANGER

No matter how irritated or infuriated you may be, never reply your boss's messages, letters, or emails when you are angry.

Every time you reply a letter in your anger, it reflects in the flow of your pen.

Your boss can sense your anger in the tone of your letter! So, no matter how mad and angry you get, resist the temptation of replying your letters or mails. Learn to stay cool. You cannot win an argument with the boss in anger.

Never forget that!

Any anger you must express must be productive and not destructive of your boss or yourself. Of what use is the anger that makes you lose your job, instead of getting promoted?

A man once told me of how his boss asked him a nasty question about the report of some board resolutions – despite the fact that he had submitted the report to the appropriate quarters. Unfortunately, because the boss spoke harshly, the man felt insulted and angrily resigned from his job. He has been living in regret ever since.

So, no matter how angry you are, save your anger for a more worthy cause. Let your anger work positively for you and not negatively.

Be careful and never try to use your anger to punish or embarrass the boss; you might be cutting off your own self.

Control yourself and never allow your anger to turn into a frenzy or hysteria.

When angry, don't be close to your boss to the extent of raising your fist against him.

No matter what you think or feel, the boss is still the master. Never reply him out of anger!

NEVER BACKSTAB THE BOSS

If you want to get to the top, never backstab your boss! Your boss is one of the steps of the ladder to the top of your career. How you treat the boss and what you say about him will determine whether your promotion will be guaranteed in a short while or prolonged in the long run.

Never oppose the boss by unlawful means like backstabbing. That is an act of disloyalty. Disloyal people never go unpunished. **Backstabbing the boss is like staging a military coup to overthrow him.**

There are no coup-plotters that go free! They are court-martialed, tried and fired! That is what happens to you managerially when you backstab the boss. No matter what you want from the management, never say things to prove how good you are and how bad the management is! No matter how disgruntled you are about the management and your boss, never do this.

- Never bad mouth your boss.
- Never engage in discussions that run down the personality of the boss.
- Never tell lies against your boss, you cannot win this fight.
- Never reveal important secrets and information about your boss's success. and career to his competitors.
- Never steal information from the boss.
- Never peek, pry or spy on the boss to know his dark secrets for the purpose of destroying him.

If you want your boss to promote you, avoid backstabbing him; go to your boss politely when you are discontented about any issue. It is more honorable for you and it can be very profitable for you! Be polite and be careful. The boss has the advantage!

Rule 50

KEEP THE BOSS'S TRUST

Trust is an invisible substance and lifestyle quality that we desire in other people towards us and which other people also desire from us.

People ask, can I trust you in on this? We are in the age of trust-breaking, disloyalty, betrayals and denials. Once the boss cannot trust you, he cannot rely on you or your word; you are seen as an unreliable and an undependable person.

The boss demands dependability and reliability from his staff or employee. **It is your duty to make yourself dependable and reliable.** Psychologist and consultant, **Jack R. Gibb** observed that, **"Trust is the result of a risk successfully survived."**

When your boss trusts you, he is taking a risk! Never make that venture a regrettable one. To foster and keep the boss's trust in you, do the following:

- Make yourself dependable.
- Keep your promise to finish certain assignments on schedule.
- Always be on time on your deadlines.
- Be recommendable.
- Be a man or woman of your word.
- Be known for honesty.
- Keep every information of the boss and company private and close to yourself, without divulging to others.
- Be trustworthy to yourself!

Shakespeare wrote, *"This above all: to thine own self be true, And it must follow, as the night the day, Thou canst not then be false to any man."*

You must be a whole person; no part of you must be broken. Be like a wedding band! No part broken or cut off!

When the boss knows you can be counted on and that your character, beliefs, and words are dependable, you will be the first to be considered for promotion. How much you can be trusted will determine how much you can be promoted.

Rule 51

CELEBRATE YOUR BOSS

Author and speaker, John C. Maxwell states, *"The true test of relationship is not only how loyal we are when friends fail, but how thrilled we are when they succeed."*

There is something good about celebrating other people's success, but there is something different, special and unique about celebrating your boss. You release new energy into his spirit that he probably never knew was there. You also release the ability of the boss to bear with you, your shortcomings and frailties.

Celebrating and praising your boss is a double plus for you. It works for the boss and it works for you! When you serve the pleasure of your boss and make him gain more energy while working with you through your positive words, praise and celebration, your career will skyrocket.

Negative words deplete energy, breed confusion, distribute disharmony, create bitterness, and trigger irritability. But praise does the exact opposite of all these! So, if you want to be promoted fast, learn to celebrate your boss! Praise him! Don't give a flattering praise or celebration; find reasons and ways to genuinely celebrate him!

Some of the ways you can celebrate your boss are:

- Talk about your boss glowingly when talking to others. Mention his name and title excitedly.
- Genuinely admire him and praise him often.
- Do something to make your boss look good especially to his boss (if he has one).
- Try to eliminate your boss's frustration.
- Praise your boss to others; they are likely to spill the beans.
- Be genuinely happy at the promotion of your boss.
- Block any loopholes or lapses around the boss
- Honor your boss's spouse.
- When the boss is traveling abroad, if you have the opportunity, see him off.
- Genuinely ask advice from him and implement it, and when it works, thank him and tell others about his expertise.

- Always make your boss a point of good reference for diligence, tolerance, love and understanding
- Save money and make money for the boss
- Find out what your boss loves - designer labels, cologne, pen etc. - and give him a surprise occasionally.

Celebrating your boss endears him to you and qualifies you for genuine promotion. You are seen as a plus, a motivator and a performer.

Here is a great counsel from Diogenes of Sinope: "A man should live with his superiors as he does with his fire: not too near, lest he burn; nor too far off, lest he freeze."

Rule 52

PRACTICE THE 101 PERCENT PRINCIPLE

The 101 percent principle, as formulated by John C. Maxwell, states: "Find the 1 percent we both agree on and give it 100 percent of your effort."

There is no gainsaying that we do not all agree on all things, but we do all agree on some things. The boss might sometimes desire you to do certain things, which might sound unethical, or which you personally might not agree with! How do you handle such a situation?

Well, you do not need to waste your time and effort quarrelling with the boss and throwing tantrums because of your opinion; rather, find one thing that you both agree on, and give it your best shot. Darryl F. Zanuck says, *"If two men on the same job agree all the time, then one is useless, if they disagree all the time, both are useless."*

Make your boss always happy by giving that one

percent idea, principally your job description, which you both agree on, your best 100% performance. Once you analyze the situation and realize that your boss and your job are worth your commitment, go ahead and do what you need to do.

Once the situation is worth it and the issue is worth your commitment, and the returns are good, go ahead and give it your best shot! What matters is not your ego, but the overall success of all - you, the boss and the entire company or organization.

The boss might not always be right, but most times he is. Why? He knows certain organizational practice and supposedly business norms, which you do not know! They are called the unwritten business rules of the company or organization. When you are known as the one who always works on agreed ideas, you are easily considered first for promotion.

Rule 53

NEVER COMPROMISE ON STANDARD WITH THE BOSS

No matter what you do - honoring the boss, celebrating the boss and treating the boss right - never try to compromise by reducing the standard of your job. Also, avoid organizational practices that can jeopardize the company's reputation.

There are good bosses - straightforward, honest, disciplined and trustworthy; and there are also shrew and crooked ones! If you happen to be working under the latter, you must be careful. When dealing with a crooked boss, never fight or reject his instructions based on what you feel is wrong or right; you cannot win that fight. Instead, **fight on principles, standard, company policy, company rules, ethics and job standard and specification.** Anything short of that, never compromise.

Where the boss is insistent, let him give you a written order for the specified instruction. If he refuses to do that, consult a higher official that is higher than both of you. Where you cannot get a respite, consult your union.

Never fight a battle you cannot win with words; fight on facts, figures and data. When you are known as a man or woman who will not compromise standard, the crooked might not promote you easily. But in the end, you will be promoted above the crooked.

Maintain standard! And get promoted later!

Rule 54

DON'T GET INTO UNNECESSARY CONFLICT WITH THE BOSS

No matter how nice you may treat the boss and protect him, conflicts are inevitable. **Conflicts are normal occurrences in life. As is often said, even your teeth and your tongue do get into conflict with each other, yet they must still get along.**

Whether you like it or not, there will be moments of misunderstanding and misinterpretation between you and your boss! You must learn how not to get into conflicts with him, however. You should also learn how to walk away from unnecessary conflicts with the boss. For instance, a topic about which car is the best in town, or which of the range of Mercedes Benz performs better than the other, can cause argument, contention and conflicts which can spill over into your job. Yet, such a discussion really has no relevance with your job.

Learn to walk away from an argument that has nothing to do with your job! **Walk away from issues that do not add value to you or your job.** Never get involved in the boss's affair with another staff member. Never take sides with your colleague against the boss. Pacify your boss when he is displeased with your colleague. Even if your colleague is right, help him to keep his cool against the boss.

Avoid unnecessary conflicts because:

It will drain you of energy and sometimes it will make you feel useless, disoriented and confused.

- It will distract you from your goals.
- It destroys your momentum and synergy with the boss.
- It will sabotage all your good work.
- It gives you a bad name and label.
- It makes others avoid working with you.
- It grounds you in one place and denies you promotion.

Avoid unnecessary conflict! Don't get into one with the boss! Walk away and have your raise!

Rule 55

RESPECT YOUR BOSS'S PRIVACY

Human beings generally love to be respected, treated specially and accorded some measure of privacy.

Our private moments, whether alone or with others, is our most precious moments to unwind and relax, recapping our moments and re-ordering our private world, thoughts, actions, plans and next line of actions. The boss's mind is a 24-hour working office. He is thinking, creating, planning and strategizing always for the general good of the corporation.

Sometimes, the boss might not have the opportunity for holidays, recreation or relaxation in a five-star hotel. What he does, instead, is to develop strategic moments of relaxation in the office. At such moments, he wants to be alone or not wanting to talk. This moment must be respected as the boss's private moment of recreation. Study these moments, know these moments, realize them and never destroy them.

You must always respect the established order of the corporation and the boss's life as an individual. To show that you respect the boss's privacy, do the following:

- Respect the responsibilities of your boss.
- Always make sure your time with the boss is appropriate for the schedule.
- Never disrespect the boss's time; speak up, speak out, and get out fast!
- **Respect your boss's private moment alone or with others.**
- Never barge into the boss's office without a knock.
- Always ask permission to speak to the boss; your time might not be right for him. Respect and observe that.
- Never stand at your boss's door to eavesdrop or to be seen as doing that.
- Treat the boss's private moments right.

Rule 56

UNDERSTAND YOUR BOSS'S TEMPERAMENT

There are several types of personality traits (known as temperaments) and it will be good for you to know where your boss belongs. Your boss's temperament determines how he acts, and it should also determine how you relate with him.

Every boss falls under one or more of the four basic temperament types:

1. **The Sanguine Boss:**

Strength	Weakness
Outgoing	Undisciplined
Charismatic	Sometimes weak-willed
Warm	Restless
Friendly	Disorganized

Responsive	Unproductive
Enthusiastic	Obnoxious and loud
Carefree	Egocentric
Compassionate	Fearful
Generous	

Deal with the sanguine boss with a lot of love, patience, understanding and swoop on him with important decisions when he is happy and calm.

2. The Melancholic Boss:

Strength	Weakness
Gifted	Moody
Analytical	Negative
Perfectionist	Critical
Investor	Rigid and Legalistic
Conscientious	Self-centered
Like a Doctor	Touchy
Philosopher	Revengeful
Artist	Persecution prone
Loyal	Unsociable
Aesthetic	Theoretical
Idealistic	Impractical

Sensitive

Self-sacrificing

Self-disciplined

Deal with the melancholic boss by not forcing yourself on him. Let him call the shots, give him advice when he asks, but never expect him to apply them.

3. The Choleric Boss:

Strength	Weakness
Leadership	Cold-Unsympathetic
Producer	Insensitive
Determined	Inconsiderate
Strong-willed	Hostile (easily angered)
Independent	Cruel and sarcastic
Decisive	Unforgiving
Practical	Self sufficient
Visionary	Domineering
Optimistic	Opinionated
Courageous	Prejudiced
Self-confident	Proud
	Crafty

Deal with the Choleric boss with a lot of patience. Listen more to him; celebrate his ideas, as he will see yours as inferior to his! Never try to challenge or compete with him. Give him loud praise! He will always think he is winning, even when you try to make him see he is losing.

4. The Phlegmatic Boss:

Strength	Weakness
Diplomat	Blasé
Calm and quiet	Sometime indolent
Easygoing	Selfish
Likeable	Stingy
Efficient	Stubborn
Organized	Self-protective
Dependable	Indecisive
Conservative	Fearful
Practical	Unmotivated
Dry Humor	

Deal with the phlegmatic boss, with a lot of persuasion. Encourage him, motivate him into action. Show him the benefits, without the problem.

If you can study your boss's temperament and understand the flow of his temperament you can always win with him, any day, any time.

Rule 57

PRAY FOR YOUR BOSS

Do you believe in the power of prayer? Yes I do! Prayer is a two-way communication. It is a communication between man and his Creator. It is a way of the mortal getting the Immortal's assistance. Prayer is a way of the natural man bringing the "super" of his Maker upon his natural ability to become supernatural.

Prayer changes things. Prayer heals, prayer helps, prayer guides, prayer strengthens. Prayer bends the hand of the wicked, and softens the heart of hardened. Prayer releases grace, peace, joy, provision, blessings and prosperity of God's divine nature on us. Prayer changes men!

John Mason said, **"Prayer might not change all things at once, but prayer changes you for all things at once."**

Cultivate the habit of prayer for your boss. The one

you pray for, you will never backstab, destroy or badmouth. The one you pray for will supernaturally feel a pull towards you.

The one you pray for will supernaturally find a pull urging him to help you, correct you, promote you and favor you.

Prayer is good for you and your boss, because prayer pleasures your own spirit and that of your Creator.

Prayer affects the lives of others around you and brings divine promotion to you and your boss! Learn to pray for your boss; it will enhance your relationship and bless your work.

Prayer plus hard work guarantees promotion!

www.ingramcontent.com/pod-product-compliance
Lightning Source LLC
Chambersburg PA
CBHW060612200326
41521CB00007B/745